POCKETBOOK

OF TIPS FOR

MOOCHERS

TERRI CORNILEUS

Author, Terri Cornileus

Pocketbook of Tips for Moochers, Copyright ©2025

Publisher, PipStones Publishing

PO Box 4507, Fort Walton Beach, Florida 32549

https://www.pipstones.com

This is a revised and updated edition. Portions of this work were previously published under earlier editions by Xlibris and PageTurner. This edition contains updated content and a newly designed cover.

Editors: Abigail Turner, Deborah Hoffman, & Elizabeth Omoh

ISBN-13: 979-8-9889427-5-7, Edition 3, Print

ISBN-13: 979-8-9889427-6-4, Edition 3, Ebook

LCCN: 2025912373 ; Copyright ©2025

Printed in the United States of America.

Dedication

I would like to dedicate this book to Ty, Mike, and my children, Troi and Jordan.

Ty, you were my muse. You drove me crazy while I was writing this book. I am sorry that your life wasn't what you expected or should have been. I hope that you stay strong, as you have the "Brown blood" running through your veins. You will persevere. What you are going through are just trials and tribulations. Believe in a higher being, God, and He will take care of you.

Mike, you were there, giving me the strength and courage to write this book. I remember talking to you about the things that were driving me wild when I had that person living with me. At times, I was irate. Then there were moments when we both laughed out loud. Thank you so much for believing in me. You let me know that I can do it. Your encouraging words and powerful hugs gave me the strength to write this book. I will never ever forget you.

Troi, you are my baby girl, my twin. This book is for you. Take heed of these words because I would be very upset if someone said my child was a Moocher. Haha. You were one of the first people that I allowed to read the unfinished product. I thought this was perfect for you as you were going off to college, and I wanted you to have a smooth transition from home to living on your own around strangers. Keep this book in your back pocket, baby girl.

Jordan, you are my dear son. Please know that I love you very much, and as a mother, there are times when we must do things that you may not like or agree with. Just know that my love for you and your sister extends to my soul, and I will never stop being your mom. As for this book, I will keep this book around our home so that you get the hint as you grow older.

Table of Contents

Introduction

Hi! I'm Terri Cornileus, and yes, I've done that thing we all swear we won't do: I let someone move in. And not just anyone, but a MOOCHER. You know, the type who shows up down on their luck, but somehow ends up down on your couch for what feels like an endless term.

Have you ever helped someone in need? Was it supposed to be temporary? Did it mysteriously turn permanent? Yes? Well, same here. That is precisely why this book exists.

Let me paint you a picture: I am divorced, with a 19-year-old daughter in college and a 13-year-old son living with his dad. I'm renting a spacious 3,200-square-foot ranch-style dream with four bedrooms, three baths, a sun porch, and designed to host my family in peace.

Then, came the phone call. A relative was in "dire straits." I was the only one with space. And before I could hang up fast enough, guilt drop-kicked me into saying yes.

Spoiler alert: **He moved in. He stayed. He got comfy. Too comfy.** What started as a kind gesture turned into a reality show called *When Moochers Attack: The Extended Stay Edition.*

At one point, my house felt less like a cozy home and more like a halfway house with better snacks. I found myself Googling things like "Can you evict someone who's never paid rent but eats all your cereal?" and "How long before squatter's rights kick in?"

So, what do you do when you're outnumbered in your own home by freeloaders with no exit plan? Well, if you're like me, you write a book.

Pocketbook of Tips for Moochers is my way of turning madness into comedy. It's for the people who've opened their doors (and fridges) to professional takers, and for the Moochers themselves. If you're going to freeload, at least be strategic about it.

We'll cover everything from what a Moocher is (you've probably met more than one) to how to recognize the signs and even how to survive or thrive, depending on which side of the couch you're on.

I use fake names to protect the guilty. But trust me, the lessons are all painfully real.

So, buckle up. Laugh out loud, and you might even want to hide your guest towels.

Happy Reading!

Throughout this book, I use fictitious names to protect the identity of various people.

Tip #1

How to Dine Without a Dime!

W ho says fine dining has to come with a bill?
With a little charm, a lot of nerve, and impeccable timing, you too can become a master of the free meal. Drop by "just to say hi" around dinnertime, gaze longingly at someone's leftovers, or casually mention how you haven't eaten all day—then watch the fridge (or menu) open like magic. Never underestimate the power of a well-timed compliment and a pitiful stomach growl.

    Food prices have skyrocketed because of the expensive economy. If you live with someone and you are unemployed with no money, you should be very cautious about how much you eat and drink. If you don't have any money to buy food, then you should not be caught in the kitchen every hour. Avoid being found with a variety of snacks and drinks under your bed or food all around you.

You were provided a temporary place to stay, not invited to an all-inclusive resort with an all-you-can-eat buffet. 3 MEALS A DAY SHOULD BE THE MAXIMUM you can gorge down on! I say this because you should not be at home eating more than you should, and consuming all your time with eating. It would be wise to be aggressively searching for employment and trying to find a permanent place to live.

If you are thirsty, drink some water. Heck, it's free! Okay? Yes, you can have some other form of liquid, but please use the same glass and DON'T, again, DON'T drink or eat the last of any item!

The last thing the head of the household wants to happen is to come home after a long day of work, anticipate eating or drinking a particular item, and find that it is gone. If this happens, BOY, ARE YOU IN TROUBLE!!!

You need to try to buy food and ask the head of the household if they need anything from the grocery store. This shows them that you understand the sacrifices they are making by letting you live there and that you are contributing to something within their house.

Try taking the initiative and scanning the refrigerator and cabinets to see what is missing or needed. Attempt to replace some of those items. The most common items that are needed are milk, butter, bread, rice, cereal, sugar, and eggs.

Everybody likes meat too! Maybe buy some meats like bacon, chicken, hamburger, or pork chops. If you really want to impress them, splurge on buying shrimp or steak. Who doesn't love a good steak (other than a vegetarian)? I KNOW I WOULD BE HAPPY!

Perhaps, you could offer the money that you were going to use to purchase the food and give it to the heads of the household. That money may be needed elsewhere, and they can use it where they see fit.

Example #1:

John was here for two weeks. He only bought groceries twice. The first week, he bought a large box of Ramen noodles, a large box of corndogs, and one tin of green tea. I am pleased that he bought food and something to snack on, but the strange thing was that he hadn't eaten any of it.

The next week, he bought some milk. I had at least 4 boxes of cereal, and he was probably annoyed with me for not buying any milk. After a long day at work, who wants to stand in line for milk? *Not me!* He bought a variety of microwave dinners and hot dogs. I was happy that he actually contributed to the household. Of course, I didn't plan on eating any of his food. That was for him to eat when he got hungry. However, sometimes it's the thought that counts. Remember, it's the little things.

Example #2:

Sharon visited every couple of months. When she was here, I was ecstatic. But you shouldn't let her into your refrigerator. She believed she could cook, eat, and drink whatever she wanted.

One day, I came home and planned to make shrimp scampi for dinner. I always made very good shrimp scampi and had been thinking about it all day. My mouth was salivating, like a dog when it's hungry or thirsty.

I got home, went to the freezer, and began to search for the shrimp. Nothing! I asked myself, *Where is that shrimp?* I knew I hadn't cooked it. I looked in the trash and found the shrimp shells.

Do you remember the Bugs Bunny and Road Runner cartoon on television? How about the times when Elmer Fudd would get so upset with Bugs Bunny that his entire face would turn red—a perfect example of me at that simmering edge! That was how I felt in that moment. Did I display my anger right then? Nope.

I turned my back and took a deep breath. I decided to go to my bedroom, wind down from the day's work, and then address the issue with Sharon afterward. I did a "don't blow up at Sharon" routine. I took off my shoes and changed into something comfortable before putting my hair up. I was cooled down.

I went to the kitchen and began to look for something else for dinner. I called Sharon into the kitchen and asked her if she had cooked the shrimp. She was a very honest person, and she admitted that she cooked them for her lunch. Now, I was thinking to myself, *Who cooks shrimp for lunch for one person?*

I'll tell ya who... Only A MOOCHER!

Anyway, I explained to her that I was going to use the shrimp for dinner and that she should ask next time. She apologized.

The point I'm trying to make isn't that she cooked and ate the shrimp. She should have called me to confirm that I didn't have plans to cook them, or to let me know that I needed to purchase more. Who doesn't get mad when someone eats or drinks the last of your favorite item? I know I do.

Signs of a Moocher:

When a person comes over to your house only at mealtime, this is a strong sign of a Moocher. When I was young, we had a family who came over daily at breakfast and dinner time. That used to make me so mad. That meant we had to share our food. When you are only getting three pieces of bacon, and now you have to share that. That meant we only got one piece. You would be mad too.

How about dinner time when your mom is cooking fried chicken, and we are guaranteed to have at least two pieces of chicken? Man, when we heard the knocking at the door, I would almost lose it, but my mom would give me that look and say, "That's family." There went my two pieces of chicken. I know now that they were Moochers.

What about a co-worker who never brings their lunch? They walk over to you and ask you what you have for lunch. So, you tell them, and what do they do? Of course, they ask for some. Before you know it, you are bringing enough food for them every day too.

What about the friend who always wants to go out to eat, but you know good and well that they don't have any money or enough money to pay for it? This person is usually the life of the party, so you invite them anyway and cover their meal.

Moocher alert!

Moocher Perspective:

1. "I don't eat that much."
2. "I am rarely here to eat."
3. "What is one more mouth to feed as long as it's not on my dime?"

Tip #2

Can I Just Use Your Phone Real Quick?

W hy waste your own minutes when someone else's phone is practically begging to be used? Whether it's a "quick call" that mysteriously lasts an hour or a borrowed phone, you treat it like your own hotline; the key is confidence.

Remember: the only thing cheaper than talk is the moocher making it.

Just because the house phone has unlimited calls does not mean that you must use and stay on the phone all day or all night. Remember, using some-one else's phone is a privilege and must not be abused. Plus, I paid for unlimited use for work and emergency purposes. The phone wasn't necessary, as I already had a cellular phone. This isn't a free phone. I may use that phone 1-2 times per week. Out of respect for the household, incoming calls should not be received after 10:00 p.m. John owns a cellphone, yet his calling plan lacks unlimited minutes

Example #1:

I went to bed around 9:00 p.m. that night, and John phoned Harriet. I woke up around 2:43 a.m. and went into the dining room to turn on the heat. I overheard John on the house phone in the family room, and he was still talking to Harriet. WHAT THE HECK? I could not believe he was still up, watching television, talking on my phone, and using my electricity. I walked away without saying anything to him to avoid losing my mind! That was a moment for biting my tongue and major self-control

I returned to bed and asked myself, *Who stays up that late at night? Who stays on someone else's phone for that long? DING! An unemployed moocher!*

Then I thought to myself, *"Why didn't you tell him to get off the phone?"* I have been told that I am very blunt, so I try to be nice, but I don't know how much I can take.

Example #2:

When I was 14 years old, I lived with my grandparents for approximately two years. Boy, did I learn a lot! I learned NOT to be a Moocher! My grandfather was very loving, but strict in his own way. God bless his soul.

When my grandfather used to catch me on the phone, he would say, "China Man, whatcha on the phone for again? Haven't you said what you wanted to say already?" I would laugh and soon hang up the phone. I didn't want my grandfather to be upset with me, nor did I want him to tell my grandmother. I learned a valuable lesson that others apparently have not.

Signs of a Moocher:

The signs point to anyone who uses your phone as their own. This person might be your family, friend, or neighbor. They will ask to use your phone quite often. You'll end up with people calling them back and even leaving voice messages for them on your own phone. Above all, they don't think about the cost of the phone or the importance of maintaining the phone line.

Moocher Perspective:

Whether I am on the phone for 10 minutes
or hours, there is no extra charge.
You have unlimited phone calls.

Tip #3

Watt the Mooch

Electricity: the silent hero of modern comfort. Lights, outlets, Wi-Fi, that mini-fridge in your room—you need it, but why pay for it when your gracious host already does? As a Moocher, your job is simple: plug in everything you own, turn on every light, and act shocked (pun intended) when the electric bill triples. Bonus points if you leave the TV on all night "for background noise" and run the AC like you're chilling meat. After all, what's a little surge in the power bill when your convenience is at stake?

When you live with someone and don't have a job, you should make sure that you don't leave any lights on. You should disconnect any appliances or games that you are not currently using. Don't turn on the ceiling fan in winter or leave the television on all night.

Everyone knows that the increase in people who live in a home, causes higher electricity bills. And naturally, there are those who have never paid a utility bill.

Example #1:

John was in the TV room, but the lights were on in the kitchen **and** his room. It was during the winter, **and** his window was wide open with the heater blaring. His reasoning was that he didn't want smoke in the house, so he had opened the window. The lights were never explained.

"TAKE YOUR BUTT OUTSIDE IN THE COLD IF YOU WANT TO SMOKE INSTEAD OF WASTING MY DARN HEAT!" Sometimes, I wonder if "the lights are on upstairs," if you know what I mean!

Example #2:

I came home, did my usual routine, and checked John's room. This became my routine because I don't like things to look messy, and I am somewhat of a neat freak. Everything must be in its place, and all beds must be made daily. Well, I noticed that John had left the bathroom light on just outside his bedroom. I was livid. I immediately called him and reminded him of the mistake. He said that he was in a rush. Then, he apologized.

Okay, I accepted his apology, but the very next day, he left that same light on AGAIN. Was I pissed? Yes, indeed! I was tempted to take the bulb out of the bathroom to teach him a lesson, but I didn't because I felt it would be wrong. I asked myself, *Who does this?* And then I answered myself, *Yep, an unemployed moocher!*

Example #3:

My grandfather did not believe that you needed to turn on the lights to walk through the house. He certainly did not approve of turning on the kitchen light at night to look into the refrigerator. First, he would shout, "Turn off that light!" and then ask, "Whatcha looking in there for again?" Then he would reassure me, "It's the same thing in there since the last time you looked."

Thinking about it now, what he said is so true. Man, I miss my grandfather!

Signs of a Moocher:

A person who **never ever** attempts to conserve energy. You leave the TV on all night, lights burning in empty rooms, or the AC/heat running non-stop. Then, at the end of the month or several months, the renter or owner must seek public assistance to pay the bill because they can't afford it, and are at risk of sitting in the dark. Is this you?

Moocher Perspective:

I don't use that much electricity, and you have to heat and cool the house anyway.

Tip #4

I Thought Water Was Free!

Water may be free when it falls from the sky, but inside a house, it comes with a price tag and a passive-aggressive stare from your host when the bill arrives. If you're a Moocher, it's your civic duty to use water like you're paying for it... even though you're not. This means no 45-minute steam room sessions in the shower and definitely no dish-by-dish faucet performances. Moochers often forget that utilities aren't powered by hopes and vibes.

Whether you're just rinsing something "real quick" or turning the washing machine into your personal waterfall, remember: every drip is draining someone else's wallet. Hydrate responsibly, or at least pretend you know how to.

If you live with someone who pays for their water, your water usage should be limited. Every time you turn that kitchen faucet on, shower, or flush that toilet, you cost that person money. When you use the washing machine, you should ensure that you use the appropriate water for that particular load. Most people say to wash clothes when you have a full load, while others say to turn the dial to low water if you have a small load.

Another thing to note is this: if you are washing the dishes, please make dish water instead of running the water and washing the dishes one at a time. Trust me, we all appreciate that you are washing the dishes, but not at the expense of increasing the water bill and using too much dish detergent. Yes, I said dish detergent. Do you know how much quality detergent costs now? Moochers, you don't, because you probably never bought any or don't remember the last time you did. Hey! Go out and buy some, and you will see. Trust me, the next time you wash dishes, you will make dish water and be frugal with the soap and water.

Example #1:

I had never seen him do dishes or even attempt to. Figure that one out.

Example #2:

Whenever I wanted to bathe, my grandfather would say, "Don't fill that tub with water." I could only fill the water up to my legs. I would wash myself and toss the water on my upper body to rinse off. We call that "having a bird bath."

Showering in his house was like jumping in and out of the tub. My grandfather wouldn't allow you to run the water for too long if you were not in the tub. You should be ready to get into the tub when you are going to take a shower. I know, sometimes, it may take a couple of minutes for the water to get hot, but once it is, take the shower.

Thinking about it now, I still like to take baths, but I see the expense and understand my grandfather's reasoning.

Signs of a Moocher:

Using your neighbor's water hose to wash your car or water your lawn. Your excuse is that you haven't made it to the hardware store to buy a water hose. Yeah, right, Moocher!

Moocher Perspective:

What? Now I can't take a bath? What about a shower? Can I at least wash my face? I didn't think it was that serious. We have to have water to live!

Tip #5

The Nicotine Ninja: How to Smoke Without Annoying Everyone!

A h, yes, the eternal struggle: house rules vs. your nicotine fix. You're a guest, not the chimney on a Victorian rooftop. If your host doesn't allow smoking indoors, don't try to negotiate. If you gotta puff, do it like a ninja—outside, quietly, and without sending the heating bill to the moon or tripping the alarm like you're breaking into Fort Knox.

Always respect the household. If smoking is not allowed in the home, do not smoke in the home, no matter what. If you get an urge to smoke in the middle of the night, go outside, but do it without disturbing the household.

Example #1:

At night, I would activate my alarm to the STAY position. My home was a non-smoking home. John was a smoker. Instead of disarming the alarm and going outside, he would open the bedroom window and stick his cigarette out the window to smoke. Who knows how many times he did this per night? THERE GOES MY HEAT! HAHA. The good thing was that he told me this was his method. I personally preferred that rather than him disarming my alarm and making my home not secure during the night.

Signs of a Moocher:

Someone who always asks for a cigarette but never buys a pack. They only purchase singles or "looseys."

Moocher Perspective:

1. What do you want from me?
2. I can go outside and smoke, but you say that I will wake you up when I disarm the alarm.
3. When I open the window and smoke, you say that I release the heat in the house. Can you give a brother a break?

Tip #6

Sneaky Sips and Crooked Blinds

Where the bottle pops and your conscience drops, welcome to Moocherville!

Rule #1: If the house doesn't allow alcohol, maybe don't treat it like your personal bar.

Rule #2: If you didn't buy it (and you're broke), maybe don't act like the party sponsor. Moochers love to drink what isn't theirs, especially when no one's looking.

Pro tip: Homeowners always know.

This area would depend on your age and the house rules. It seems to me that if you don't have a job, how could you afford to purchase or drink alcohol, especially someone else's? Some households have a no-drinking policy. If that's the case, please respect their wishes and do not drink in their home.

Example #1:

I had a party at my house, and had leftover cans of beer in a metal beer bucket that were still on my sun porch. I am not a beer drinker, so the beers had stayed out there for a while. When my relatives found out that the beer was out there, some of them would "visit" while I was out and about. They would sneak out to my back porch and help themselves. They would actually go out and grab some beers, sneak around, and drink them, thinking I wouldn't know. Can you believe that?

What they forgot or didn't know is that I am a neat freak and like everything to be in its place. I noticed that the blinds leading to the sun porch were in disarray, and I immediately knew they had been guzzling them down. GUESS WHAT? I FIXED THEM! I then took all of the beers and hid them. THERE IS NO NEED TO PENALIZE EVERYONE BUT THE MOOCHERS.

Example #2:

In my "past life," I had another party at my home in which some of the guests stayed over. We had an entertainment center that had a bar section. It was located in our partial basement. We kept our alcohol there. One of our guests spent the night and slept in the basement. We woke up the next morning to find out that a large portion of the alcohol had been consumed by them. We were shocked! Who would take the liberties as a guest and drink another person's alcohol? You know the answer already. I won't even say it!

Example #3:

I went to a cookout at someone's house, and they have a "No-Drinking" policy. There were actually guests drinking alcohol in the garage and outside the house. I kid you not. Now, I know you will say that drinking was not allowed in the house, but you know that it was wrong for those guests to do that. They had no respect for the homeowner.

The homeowner finally made it clear that drinking alcohol in **and** around her home would not be tolerated.

If you must drink, drink in moderation outside the home if drinking is not allowed in the house. AS ALWAYS, DO NOT DRINK AND DRIVE!

Signs of a Moocher:

Anyone who drinks alcohol while they are broke. They have no problem diving into a liquor cabinet and drinking up the old, unopened bottles. All alcohol is theirs for the taking.

Moocher Perspective:

1. What's a little alcohol among friends? Caring is sharing!
2. She said no drinking in her house, so I drank against the wall on the outside of the house.
3. They offered me some alcohol earlier in the day. I just drank more when they were asleep. I didn't know there was a limit.

Tip #7

Guests of Guests Are NOT Blessed

You're already mooching. This isn't the time to become a cruise director. Bringing extra people into someone else's home without permission is next-level disrespect.

Hint: your host doesn't want to feed or house your cousin, your boo, or your "ride."

Questions like this should not be going through my mind when I come home from a long day's work. *Can you have a guest over? Really? You're already a guest! How dare you invite people over to use someone else's water, food, electricity, and everything else!* ASK FOR

PERMISSION! Whether you are a kid or older, it is not your home and is only a temporary residence, so be respectful.

If you must have guests, please limit it to a few, and don't make it a revolving door. This is not a hotel.

Example #1:

I arrived home from working all day to find Tom, Dick, John, and Harry in my family room (let's call them that for now). Some men were playing pool while others were playing Xbox Live. They all had something to drink, and snacks were scattered about.

They could tell I was bothered as they all went outside to smoke cigarettes. Did I lose my cool? Absolutely! I took all of the pool table sticks and hid them. Some people may think or say that it is childish, but everybody knows that a Moocher will do things in your home that they normally would not do when you are there.

I am out working every day, and when I come home, I don't have time to play pool or want to entertain anyone. Now, if it were already planned, then that would be different. Does the Moocher have time to entertain and play pool? Absolutely! He was playing pool all day and night. NOT ANYMORE!

Do I want any guests over? Not all the time. If John does not respect my home, why would I think he would insist that his guest respect my home? I am a private person, and I don't want everyone in my house. Plus, if it weren't for this situation, he wouldn't be in my home as much as he is. At this point, I have no privacy!

Signs of a Moocher:

This type of person only visits to obtain the benefits of several things, like eating, drinking, partying, and sleeping. They come over often and do not contribute financially. Again, they are fun to hang around, but eventually, you'll notice they are around too much.

Moocher Perspective:

They should be grateful I want to come over. After all, I am the life of the party.

Tip #8

This Ain't a Sleepover, Skippy!

Moochers love a good "I'll just crash here tonight" moment. But when "a night" turns into an uninvited extended stay, congratulations—you and YOUR overnight guest now live rent-free in creating someone else's nightmare.

I wish they would try to have an overnight guest. There's no need to ask or suggest. The answer will always be, "HECK NO!" Only the heads of the household will have overnight guests. Even in that case, there is a limit to the number of days that they are allowed to stay. It pays to be the boss in this house.

Signs of a Moocher:

This person tends to visit only in the evenings and eventually falls asleep on the couch. In case you hear a moocher knocking on the door, don't hide and pretend you can't hear them:

Answer the door, and just say it.

"NO!"

"NOT TONIGHT!"

No explanation needed. No guilt. No stress.

Moocher Perspective:

I like spending the night here. It offers the comforts of a hotel without the expense of paying for one. I receive a room, meals, and entertainment for free. What a deal!

Tip #9

Manifesting a Job While Earning a Gold Medal in Napping

The "job hunt" looks suspiciously like binge-watching TV, leaving dishes in the sink, and taking three-hour naps. But every time you ask, they say, "I'm still searching." *Mmm hmm.*

Looking for employment should be a daily task and a high priority. You should explore all means of communication for employment, including newspapers, the internet, and drive-bys. You should inform the heads of the household that you are actively searching for employment. The time to select a job based on salary or title is over.

You need to find a job ASAP! Then, find a place to live ASAP! Time is of the essence. You no longer have the liberty to pick and choose the ideal job and the perfect place to live. You must accept anything that is legal until you can find something better.

Example #1:

There are approximately 20 stores within walking distance of my home. John applied to one store. I told him on several occasions that he needed to submit an application to almost all of them. He told me that he was going to follow up with the only store that he applied to. He has been telling me this for two weeks. His version of "follow up" must be very different from mine. Mine requires getting up from the couch and walking out the door. His idea must be grabbing another bag of chips and watching his favorite show. One thing was sure: I was losing my patience. Someone needed to come to my rescue quickly!

Signs of a Moocher:

Anyone who expects an immediate job hook-up because their relative or friend is a business owner.

Moocher Perspective:

We are family. Family helps each other.

Tip #10

Quiet Hour Applies to Moochers Too

Believe it or not, your host's home isn't open 24/7 like a convenience store. Moochers have a way of ignoring household rhythms and treating every hour like "their time."

Returning home at an unreasonable time is disrespectful when you live with someone. If you are going out and know you will be back extremely late (3–4 a.m. or later), you should make other sleeping arrangements. Coming into the house very late is simply rude! If you live in an area with no street lights, and it is very quiet, any noise is disturbing and could wake up the household members or the neighbors.

Example #1:

John came home at 4:00 a.m. There was noise from the alarm when he disengaged it. Then, lo and behold, light beamed from the kitchen. And, of course, there was noise from the refrigerator, water running from the faucet, and the microwave door opened and closed several times. I tried to hold my composure and hoped that he would hurry out of the kitchen, but when I heard the microwave door closing again, I knew I had to say something to him. I went into the kitchen and explained to him that it was very late and that he was waking up the household. He told me he was trying to make as little noise as possible.

I was taught that if you spend the night at someone else's house, you should come in at a certain time. If you are going out and you will be back late, then you should arrange alternate lodging unless you are going out with the person who pays the bills, rents the house, or owns the house. Therefore, there would be no one to disturb when you enter the home late.

I think the same rules should apply, especially if you are not a household contributor. I am used to living alone. I am a light sleeper. I am very picky about my safety and who and when someone enters or exits my home. Plus, I can make the rules because I AM THE BOSS OF THIS HOUSE!

Signs of a Moocher:

Any person who comes into the home at an unreasonable hour and refuses to abide by the house rules. This person is also disrespectful. They feel they are grown and, therefore, can do what they please.

Moocher Perspective:

I'm a grown man! I mean no disrespect. I will try not to make any noise when I come in at night, other than the alarm, the microwave, the fridge, and water running. Well, it's hard to be quiet, okay?

Tip #11

The Lazy Guest Chronicles

M oochers treat cleaning like a foreign concept. They can find the remote, your Wi-Fi password, and the snack drawer, but not the broom, mop, or trash can.

No one should have to ask you or remind you to clean up your room or the space that you occupy. That should be understood. Not only should you keep your room clean, but you should also volunteer to clean another area of the house. If you took the initiative and cleaned the kitchen, you would make someone very happy. After all, you are in their home more than the homeowners and use more dishes than they do.

Example #1:

I walked past Sean's room, and a stench slapped my nose. I looked around as I tried to determine where the smell was coming from. There I was, sniffing around the area like a dog. My nose ended up at the doorway of Sean's room. I knocked on the door, and Sean opened it. The smell that oozed from his room almost knocked me over backward. At this point, he was looking at me crazily. I asked him what the smell was, and he said he couldn't smell anything. Is it true that a person can get accustomed to their environment, thus a scent? Well, the room was stinky, like bedding would be after a century in a dragon's lair. I was livid. He doesn't pay any bills. The least he can do is clean up the room. Heck, open the windows and let some fresh air in.

Pointer: This is not a hotel; you sure don't have a maid. Clean up the darn room!

Signs of a Moocher:

This person is given their own room, a bathroom, plenty of food to eat, and a laundry room to wash their clothes. They don't pay any bills. They are asked to keep their room clean and wash their clothes. Do they do this? No! They act like they are entitled to have these things. They look at you like you have asked them to do a menial task.

Moocher Perspective:

It looks clean to me, but you know, some people just like things a different way. It smells fine, too. Maybe your nose is just sensitive.

Tip #12

Cash Me If You Can!

"I meant to pay you back. It's just... life has been hard. And by life, I mean my shoe addiction and daily coffee habit."

One of the things a Moocher does will be to ask for money. Do they ask for a minimal amount of money? Sometimes, they do, but I have been asked for hundreds and hundreds of dollars from a Moocher. Should you let a Moocher borrow money? Let's get this straight. Think of it this way, if they are a Moocher and live with you, do they really have the money to pay you back, especially if it's a large amount? No. I think it is ridiculous for a Moocher to ask for money. They know they are living off of you for free and have no way to pay it back or even in the near future.

There will be times when you may need to loan them money to get to an interview or even purchase the clothes they need. We all know people who do not have the proper clothes or transportation to go for an interview.

Let's keep it real, though. Are we really expecting to be paid back by the Moocher? Yes and no. Yes, I would love to get all my money back plus interest; however, I am told that if you loan someone money, you should not expect it back. Personally, I think that is bull crap. I am not a bank, nor am I a check-cashing place. I want and need my money back. Frankly, they should want to work to pay you back. There's honor in that.

Example #1:

John came to live with me. I took the initiative and purchased him the basics, like a toothbrush, toothpaste, soap, and toilet paper for his bathroom. I noticed he had been wearing the same clothes—for several days. I asked him if he had extra clothes, and he said, "No." I went out and talked to some family members and obtained some clothing for John. Ok, they were not new, but they were free. It was during the winter, and he didn't have a winter coat. I found him a coat as well. Was he grateful? Nope. He gave the coat to another relative of ours.

I had given him money for a variety of things. At the time, I did not expect anything back. If he offered me money, I most definitely would have taken it, though. I think if you ask for money, you should pay it back someday, no matter what happens (other than dying with no life insurance).

People tend to believe that if a long period of time passes by and the person who gave you the money doesn't ask for it, then you don't have to worry about paying it back. Again, that is bull crap. YOU OWE IT, NOW PAY IT! If you keep your word, that person will likely let you borrow money again when you need it most.

Signs of a Moocher:

1. If you are that person, possibly a friend, who always wants to go somewhere, and you know that you do not have any money, but you are the first person to jump in the car, then you are a Moocher.

2. If you text a person and ask to borrow money, you are a Moocher.

3. If you ask for money to pay for your entertainment and wants, you are a Moocher!

4. If you ask for money to buy cigarettes and alcohol and to get your hair, nails, and toes done, you are a Moocher.

If you are borrowing money, you are still a Moocher. When you ask to borrow money, it should be for something important or an emergency. Do you realize you are taking that money from another person's income and their needs?

Moocher Perspective:

You are selfish. All that money you have—you know, you can't die with it. It's just money.

Tip #13

Driven to Mooch

You know it's bad when your guest knows your car better than you. Moochers love to "borrow" your vehicle like it came with the guest room. Gas tank empty. Seat adjusted. You? Annoyed.

Have you heard this question before?... "Can I borrow your car? I will buy you gas." Gas? Gas? What about my monthly car payment? My car insurance? What about the additional mileage that you would put on my car? Who is going to pay for the maintenance of my vehicle? Your paying for gas doesn't cover the expenses of using this car.

Before you even think about tossing your keys to someone, ask a few basic questions:

1. Do you have a valid driver's license?

2. Is it suspended?

3. Got warrants?

4. When was the last time you hit something (or someone)?

And if you're the one asking to borrow a car, just know that "I'll put gas in it" doesn't magically erase the risk, cost, or paperwork the owner would be stuck with if things go sideways.

Example #1:

Your cousin swings by "just for a minute," then casually asks, "Hey, mind if I borrow your car real quick? Just to run to the store?" Fast forward 45 minutes; they're still gone. When they finally come back, the seat is pushed all the way back, the radio is blasting some station you've never heard of, your air freshener is missing, and they somehow managed to bring back no groceries. But don't worry—they toss you $2 and say, "That's for gas."

Signs of a Moocher:

They **always** ask to borrow your car, but never offer to help with actual maintenance. They magically "lose" their license when it's time to show it. They have a long, dramatic story involving tickets, towing, or "bad luck" that explains why they don't have a car. They consider your ride their backup plan—but never own up to their responsibilities. The only time they offer you money is when it's in the form of change from your own cupholder.

Moocher Perspective:

Who could afford all of those expenses? That's why I borrow other people's cars. I'll just put some gas in it. Or they only offer you money in the form of change from your own cupholder.

Tip #14
Freeload Express

Moochers LOVE a free ride, especially when you're already going their way. Suddenly, your passenger seat is reserved, and your gas tank is suffering in silence.

What does carpooling mean? It's an arrangement whereby several participants travel together in one vehicle. They share the costs of travel and often take turns as the driver. Well, I once tried this with a co-worker. We worked for the same company, had the same supervisor, and lived in the same community. We both had very nice, working vehicles. This was a perfect arrangement where we could both save money. He drove me to work one time. I drove him to work so many times that I lost count.

I am a strong-minded individual, and I don't have a problem saying "No!" This person would text me early in the morning and, in a roundabout way, demand a ride, not ask. He would say, "Can I get a ride with you? Thank you."

I, on the other hand, felt like I was being used. Do I need a travel buddy in the morning? Nope. Well, after so many texts like that, I started ignoring them. Finally, I said, "No!"

If you must carpool, you must take turns driving your own vehicle, too. No one should feel used and unappreciated. An arrangement was made, and you should keep up with your end of the bargain.

Signs of a Moocher:

A person who asks for a ride somewhere but rarely contributes to the cost. They assume they are entitled because they know you and because you are going to the same place. Free Uber service!

Moocher Perspective:

1. My car is leased, and I can't put that many miles on it.
2. We are going to the same place anyway.
3. What does another person in the car matter? Nothing. It costs you nothing to let me ride with you.

Tip #15

Saving Money by Mooching Off Yours

S aving money is great. Moochers do it by spending none of theirs and all of yours. They're living rent-free, eating for free, and somehow stashing coins like a dragon guarding treasure.

When you live with someone, they tell you that you don't need to pay any bills. They aren't just being nice; the expectation is for you to save your money. You never know when your time is up. When the time comes, you should be able to move out and have enough money to pay for a hotel or other suitable place.

Example #1:

Cordell told his mother that he had money in the bank. She found out that he actually had no money in there. Instead of saving his money, he had purchased an Xbox and other frivolous items.

Signs of a Moocher:

This aligns with someone who refuses to save their money and feels like they won't get kicked out when they contribute nothing.

Moocher Perspective:

My parents will never kick me out.
I am their child.

What's Next for the Moocher?

C ongratulations!

You've made it to the end of the Moocher Manual. If you've read this far without getting defensive, slamming the book shut, or storming off to sulk in someone else's guest room, there might be hope for you yet. Now's the time for reflection, redemption, and maybe, just maybe, a little personal responsibility. Ask yourself: What can I do not to get kicked out? Better yet, how can I stop being a full-time freeloading, energy-draining, food-snatching house ghost? Don't worry, we're not leaving you to figure it out alone. Below is your Moocher Morning-to-Night Survival Guide, because personal growth is real, and eviction notices are too.

Moochers, you should ask yourself, "What could I do to make my living here peaceful?" Well, if you don't know, I will tell you. After reading this book, you will no longer be a Moocher!

MORNING:

Get up and ask the heads of the household if there is anything you need to do. If they tell you to do something, make sure you do it because if you don't, you are in BIG TROUBLE.

If they don't have anything for you to do, say this, "If you change your mind, just call me," and then follow with a nice, "HAVE A GOOD DAY!"

Now, you can get back in bed for another 1-2 hours and not have them talk about you because you are lying in their bed, in their home, while they are leaving for work to pay for the house and utilities you are using freely.

Some may wonder why I said they should return to bed for another 1-2 hours. I said that because if they remain awake, they will use the electricity and eat the food. Also, I get up every day at 5:30 a.m.

Moocher Perspective:

I am going to stay in the room. Out of sight is out of mind.

MID–AFTERNOON:

By this time, you should have researched a job and gone out and applied/completed at least 1-2 job applications, even if they do not have a sign outside their window stating, "HIRING."

If you get home before the head of the household, do something, anything around the house. There is cleaning, mopping, sweeping, watering the plants, or preparing dinner. Do something that will lessen the pressure off you and the strain off of them.

Another thing you could do is outside work. Cut the grass, trim the trees, or clean the windows. Do something to show your appreciation.

Moocher Perspective:

I will make some phone calls today and make the appointments for later this week.

NIGHT:

People who do not typically work often sleep during the day and stay up all night to socialize. I have encountered individuals in this situation firsthand. You tend to leave the house when the heads of the household are coming home and return late at night when they believe everyone is asleep. I have heard that you are trying to show that you rarely spend time at home and do not consume food or use electricity. If that is your mindset, then you should consider MOVING OUT!

Coming in at a decent time during the night shows respect. Most households shut down in preparation to rest for the next work day. No one is telling you to come in the house at 8:oo p.m. or 9:oo p.m., but it is a sign of respect if you come in at a decent time of the night and don't cause disruption in the home.

Moocher Perspective:
I am done for the day.

WEEKENDS:

Moochers should get up early on Saturday morning. Going out and purchasing the newspaper to look for a job is a great idea. If you don't have a car, try to schedule your job search within the same vicinity. That way, whoever is dropping you off does not have to wait around for you to take you to the different job locations. Please arrange your own transportation. The last thing the heads of the household want to do is get up early on a Saturday morning to take you to look for a job. Will they be happy that you are looking for a job? Yes, but not at their expense.

You should also consider arranging to stay somewhere else on the weekend. This should give the heads of the household some space and privacy. If you decide to do this, just let them know and ask if there is anything they need to do and if they need some alone time. I believe they would appreciate that.

Moocher Perspective:

1. If you are off from work, so am I.
2. I need to rest.
3. I am tired of looking for a job.

Final Thoughts (a.k.a. Your Last Warning)

So here we are at the end of the road. If this book made you laugh, cringe, or reflect on just how much food you've eaten that wasn't yours, good. That was the goal. Being a Moocher isn't a permanent condition. It's a choice. And now you have the tools, the perspective, and the slightly bruised ego to make better ones. Will you continue living like the world owes you a couch, the internet, and coffee? Or will you finally stand up (after sleeping in, of course) and do better? Either way, if you've been reading this while staying in someone else's house, go do the dishes. Like, now!

You're welcome.

Epilogue

My "tough love" worked and I reclaimed my home!

I told the Moocher that he had one month to find employment so that he could pay for his auto insurance. Where I lived, you could have a problem getting a good job, if you didn't have a car.

Guess what? He found a job within three weeks of moving into my house. I was on him every day, and I am here to say, my methods worked! I constantly had to ask him, "Did you look for a job? Where did you go? What did they say? Did you follow up with them again? Why are you still in the house? Is it time to get up?" I sort of felt like a broken record with several cracked layers, but again, he had success finding employment.

From that point on, he had two to three months to find a place to live. That may seem like short notice, but time was of the essence, and so was my sanity.

I was trying to teach him not just some responsibility but also basic life skills. To the best of my knowledge, those time frames were sufficient to complete the extent of "moochiness."

I had already explained my expectations to John when he moved here, and I emphasized that it was only a temporary arrangement until he found a permanent place to live. I also believe anyone can make any place a home. John is young, single, and without children. Does he need a two-bedroom apartment? Does he really need a one-bedroom apartment? If he can't afford it, then the answer is "NO."

With that in mind, it's the little things that count. People need to stop living above their means. A studio apartment is good enough. You can't expect the Lap of Luxury Homes International to be your next step. Start small and expand when you can afford it.

Moochers don't understand how much stress they cause people. It is even more difficult to handle if they are your children or a family member. To me, Moochers are parasites. It feels like they are sucking the very life from you and depleting your saving accounts at the same time.

Moochers, I have one last crucial tip for you.

Don't get an attitude when you move out!

You never know when you may need that person or have to move back in!

I hope this book, ***Pocketbook of Tips for Moochers,*** will help the Moocher in you and those who were victims of your charades and escapades.

And... Happy Savings!

Biography

Terri Cornileus

Terri and her twin brother were born on February 6, 1968, in Rockledge, Florida. The two were inseparable—bound by the unique closeness only twins share. But in 1973, when they were just five years old, tragedy struck. Terri's twin passed away. Her other half was gone. That moment changed everything. Terri became withdrawn, and her entire view of the world shifted. In an effort to comfort and demonstrate love to her, Terri's family spoiled her.

When Terri was 14, her grandmother extended an invitation to live with her and Terri's grandfather in New Jersey. After some thought, she decided to go—and that decision became a turning point.

In New Jersey, she learned about rules, expectations, discipline, and grace. Her mother and grandmother taught her how to speak with poise, dress with purpose, and carry herself well in social settings. Her grandfather, full of wisdom and wit, taught her the importance of character, while interactions with her aunts and uncles helped her realize that life is much bigger than ourselves.

That home gave Terri what she calls "a new life." She began to expect more from herself. She enlisted in the Army and served for eight years. It was a perfect fit. Her military career brought order and pride, and she continues to honor that legacy through active in-volvement in veterans' organizations like the Ameri-can Legion.

After leaving the military, a friend's mother intro-duced her to the insurance world. Terri became a licensed auto appraiser and later a senior claims ad-juster, holding licenses in several states. Her career grew alongside her creativity—Terri also has a pas-sion for interior decorating and finds joy in creating beautiful, peaceful living spaces.

Terri is also a proud mother to a daughter and a son, both of whom are now grown and thriving in their own lives. Watching them navigate adulthood has deepened her understanding of the challenges young people face and the importance of finding meaning and direction.

Terri wrote her book as a message to those who've lost their way—especially young people who don't yet see the value in themselves or the direction in their lives. Through her writing, she hopes to help them appreciate their families, their friends, and the gifts they've been given. It's a reminder that even when life feels rocky, there's still hope and purpose, and sometimes, we all just need a little nudge to find it.

Follow Terri Cornileus @:

Facebook: Author Terri Cornileus

Instagram: moochers_tip

TikTok: terri.cornileus

PipStones Publishing

"Weavers of Tales and Tellers of Truth"

Mission Statement:
Our mission is to publish unique and refreshing works from various authors and genres; to present and highlight literary endeavors in an ever-changing marketplace.

Services:
Editing, Formatting, Illustrations, Publishing, Distribution, Local & Social Marketing, Author Coaching

Note to an Author:
Reach out for a free author consultation:
https://www.pipstones.com/booking-calendar
and follow our social media for more book news and information!

Facebook: @pipstonespublishing
Instagram: @pipstones
TikTok: @pipstonespublishing
X: @pip_stones

<u>Purchase Our Newest Book</u>
Now What?:
The 7 Vital Steps to Self-Publish your Manuscript

Now What? Book